WOMEN OF THE BIBLE

Old Testament

Rose Visual Bible Studies

Women of the Bible: Old Testament
Rose Visual Bible Studies

©2021 Rose Publishing

Published by Rose Publishing
An imprint of Tyndale House Ministries
Carol Stream, Illinois
www.hendricksonrose.com

ISBN 978-164938-027-2

All rights reserved. No part of this work may be reproduced or transmitted in any form or by any means, electronic or mechanical, including photocopying, recording, or by any information storage and retrieval system, without permission in writing from the publisher.

Author: Cyndi Parker (PhD, University of Gloucestershire) teaches in seminaries, universities, and churches around the world. Cyndi is the Professor of Holy Land Studies at the Israel Bible Center and an adjunct professor at Jerusalem University College. She hosts the Context Matters podcast and publishes papers focused on the cultural and geographical context of the Bible. Cyndi lived in Jerusalem for five years, has led dozens of trips to Israel, and continues to develop innovative, educational trips that inspire students of all ages through experiential education.

Special thanks to Rachel Asproth for use of her poem, "A Prayer for Women: Remember Your Daughters." This poem first appeared in the Summer 2017 issue of CBE's *Mutuality* magazine (www.cbeinternational.org).

Scriptures taken from the Holy Bible, New International Version®, NIV®. Copyright © 1973, 1978, 1984, 2011 by Biblica, Inc.™ Used by permission of Zondervan. All rights reserved worldwide. www.zondervan.com The "NIV" and "New International Version" are trademarks registered in the United States Patent and Trademark Office by Biblica, Inc.™

Scripture quotations marked NLT are taken from the Holy Bible, New Living Translation, copyright ©1996, 2004, 2015 by Tyndale House Foundation. Used by permission of Tyndale House Publishers, a Division of Tyndale House Ministries, Carol Stream, Illinois 60188. All rights reserved.

Images used under license from Shutterstock.com: Cover photo, p. 5; Noel Powell, p. 3, 7; Javarman, p. 8, 22, 38, 52, 54, 68, 82, 96; James William Smith, p. 12; Guitarfoto, p. 3, 21; Kavram, p. 26; Matyas Rehak, p. 27; ER_09, p. 3, 37; Tsekhmister, p. 47; Paopano, p. 3, 53; vvvita, p. 55; Lisa Mar, p. 3, 67; Rocketclips, Inc., p. 3, 81; Melinda Raduly, p. 83; Antonina Vlasova, p. 87; Chat Karen Studio, p. 3, 97; P Maxwell Photography, p. 98, 108, 109; amenic181, p. 101; Keep Smiling Photography, p. 103.

Eliezer and Rebekah in Dalzierls' Bible Gallery (c. 1865–1881); *Rebecca Meets Isaac by the Way* by James Tissot (c. 1896–1902), p. 14; *The Daughters of Zelophehad* in *Bible Pictures* by Charles Foster (1897), p. 23; *Jael and Sisera* by Jacopo Amigoni (c. 1739), p. 39; Jezreel Valley and Gezer photos by Cyndi Parker, p. 41, 85; *Jael Shows to Barak, Sisera Lying Dead* by James Tissot (c. 1896–1902), p. 45; Tel Abel Beth Maacah photo by Moshechn/Wikimedia.org, p. 60; Mt. Carmel/Wikimedia.org, p. 69; Shunem photo by www.HolyLandPhotos.org, p. 71; *Elisha Raising the Shunammite's Son* by Benjamin West (1766), p. 75; Relief maps by Michael Schmeling, www.aridocean.com.

Printed in the United States of America
020822VP

Contents

"Charm is deceptive, and beauty is fleeting; but a woman who fears the LORD is to be praised"

Proverbs 31:30

Women of the Old Testament

There are over one hundred women who are named in the Old Testament, and many more who are in the narratives but remain unnamed. Some of these women held significant leadership roles in their communities, while others led a more quiet life. Stories about women are not as plentiful in the Bible as the ones about men, and yet, women played important roles in the unfolding story of biblical history. Their stories deserve our careful attention.

The biblical writers do not give us all the details we might want about these women's background, family life, thoughts, and desires. Instead, we are shown more of a snapshot of these women than an opportunity to follow them through all stages of life. Yet their stories are preserved in the Bible for a reason. So ponder these narratives and reflect on what we can learn about God by paying attention to these women.

This study highlights six stories of women from different Old Testament time periods. We start with Rebekah, one of Israel's earliest matriarchs, and then we consider five sisters who influenced the Israelite law code while the Israelites wandered in the wilderness. Among the tribes of Israel who entered the land of promise, we meet a national leader in Deborah and a feisty non-Israelite warrior in Jael. From the time period of the Israelite monarchy, we examine the lives of two women whose names have been lost in history. Finally, we conclude with Lady Wisdom from the book of Proverbs.

In this study, we'll ask questions of the women in the biblical text:

- Do we know their names?
- Where did they live?
- What was life like for them?
- What cultural expectations did they honor, and which ones did they challenge?

You may encounter women who encourage you, or maybe they frustrate you. Perhaps you have heard some of these stories before, but some will likely be unfamiliar. When you get to the unfamiliar stories, ask yourself why you don't know them. Is it because you are new to the Bible? Or maybe your church doesn't teach these narratives? When we skip over biblical stories, we lose a portion of the narrative of how God interacts with diverse people in society.

Bring an attitude of curiosity into these lessons. Explore the lives of people who lived in a different place, during a different time period, and with different cultural expectations from your own. Despite the differences, these women knew the same God you are studying now. Can we see the story of God through the eyes of Old Testament women with the eyes of modern women? By asking that question, we will discover more about the God of the Bible and our own transformative roles in God's larger narrative.

1 REBEKAH

A Matriarch in the Making

Rebekah

Much of the book of Genesis is focused on Abraham, Isaac, and Jacob, who were the patriarchs of the family God chose to work through to bring hope and restoration to the world. But woven into four chapters in the middle of Genesis (chapters 24–27) is the story of the great matriarch, Rebekah. These chapters give us an unusual glimpse into what life was like for Rebekah—from the time she meets Abraham's servant at the well, through twenty years of infertility, to helping her son Jacob receive the coveted blessing of the firstborn. Rebekah emerges as a primary character in these chapters of the story of God's people.

In this session, we'll focus on Rebekah's character in her early years. We meet her for the first time when she goes to a well to collect water and encounters someone from a faraway place. The man was a servant of Abraham, Rebekah's relative. The servant was on a quest to find a wife for Abraham's son Isaac. Would Rebekah take the risk of leaving everything she knew behind to become the wife of Isaac, a man she had never met, and become the new matriarch of Abraham's family in a distant land?

Read It

Key Bible Passage

For this session, read Genesis 24:1–67.

Optional Reading

Rebekah's infertility and pregnancy: Genesis 25:19–26

Rebekah's role in the blessing of Jacob: Genesis 27:1–46

As you read, pay attention to the details given in the narrative, like how Rebekah's character is set in contrast to her brother's, or how she talks about her family home. When does Rebekah speak and when is she not heard? Consider the characteristics necessary to be invited to become the new matriarch of Abraham's family.

"Before [the servant] had finished praying, Rebekah came out with her jar on her shoulder."

GENESIS 24:15

Know It

1. List the actions Rebekah takes in the following verses in Genesis 24. Consider how this helps us understand her role in the story?

   Verse 18: ______________________________

   Verse 20: ______________________________

   Verse 28: ______________________________

   Verse 58: ______________________________

   Verses 64–65: ______________________________

2. Abraham gave his servant a monumental task, to choose the next matriarch. Pay attention to the servant's prayer (Gen. 24:12–14). What might he have been looking for in the character of the woman he would choose to be Isaac's wife?

3. What are some questions this story brings up for you—especially about cultural customs, how the characters interact, and what they do?

Culture

Ancient societies were organized around a *patriarchal* structure in which the family identity was defined by the father of the house. Such societies were often *patrilocal* as well. This means that when two families joined through marriage, the woman moved into the man's house with his extended family. Each of these elements sit in the background of Rebekah's story. The patriarch Abraham was the head of the household, and from his two sons, God chose Isaac to inherit the promises of the covenant God made with Abraham (Gen. 12). Abraham lived in Canaan but did not want a Canaanite wife for his son Isaac. Since Abraham and his wife Sarah had both come from Mesopotamia, that is where he sent his servant to find a wife for his son. The patrilocal element is evident in the story, as we see it's assumed that Rebekah would leave her homeland to join Isaac where he lived.

Rebekah's narrative gives us a view of life for women at that time. Many Old Testament stories focus on the public sphere—like royal courts, military campaigns, and civic issues—where men had more authority than women. We do not often see inside the home to consider all that women did. Recent studies in archaeology and anthropology emphasize the real influence women had in their communities. Males were the head of the household who provided the public face for the family, but women created unseen networks

Patriarchal: A family organized around the authority and privilege of the oldest living male.

Patrilocal: A concept of living space centered around the male members of the family. The woman moves into her husband's house after marriage.

that sustained the community. Women shared work, cared for each other's families, supplied medical aid for the sick, and created goods that were sold to support their families. As we follow Rebekah's story, we move from the public space at the well into the private space of her family home.

Geography

Rebekah's story is situated in two vastly different geographical arenas: Mesopotamia and the biblical Negev. Mesopotamia benefited from the Tigris and Euphrates rivers that provided a constant source of water and fertile soil. It was a well-resourced land with international connections. The Negev, on the other hand, was a marginal land without a reliable water source, except the rain from heaven, which, at most, only totaled twelve inches a year. The type of soil covering the ground created a hard, thin crust that required constant breaking apart so the rain could soak into the ground. The limited rain meant farmers could grow cereal crops like wheat and barley, but the dryness pushed most residents to also raise sheep and goats. Like a frontier land, the region was promising, but it was also very dangerous. In our story, we watch in awe as Rebekah chooses to leave the easier lands of Mesopotamia to join her future husband in the Negev.

Tel Arad, an archaeological site in the northern Negev, with a walled Canaanite city and fortress

Time Line

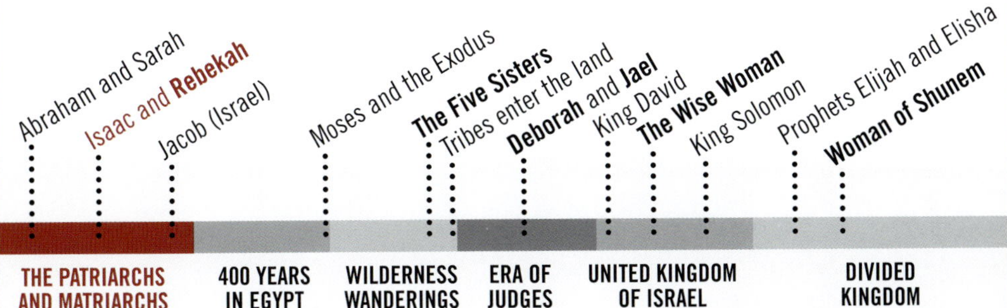

Narrative

Genesis 24 opens with an aged Abraham sending his trusted servant to Mesopotamia to accomplish a daunting task. The servant was to find a relative from Abraham's family tree who was a suitable spouse for Abraham's son, Isaac. As the servant completed the long journey to Mesopotamia, he stopped at a well on the outskirts of a town. His decision was practical, because as an outsider to the area, the well was where he could make helpful contacts. Wells were also the local gathering places for young unmarried youth who were often tasked with minding the flocks. If you wanted to find the marriageable young women and gain some information about the local surroundings, the well was the perfect place to go (a decision also made by Jacob and Moses in Genesis 29:1–14 and Exodus 2:15–22).

When the servant arrived at the well, he prayed an earnest and dramatic prayer for God's chosen woman to not only offer him water to drink, but also to offer water for his camels. Even by modest estimates, a camel can drink more than twenty gallons of water at a time, with each gallon weighing over eight pounds. For any young woman to fulfill the servant's requirement, she would have to pull up more than two hundred pounds of water for each of his ten camels (Gen. 24:10). Basically, the servant was asking God to let the young woman be a superhero—or at least someone with a deep-seated character of selfless generosity. Although the story doesn't say what the servant's motivation was for this unique request, it's quite possible he knew that these characteristics were essential for a future matriarch, because they were characteristics Abraham himself displayed (Gen. 18).

When Rebekah enters the scene, only the reader is told of her patriarchal lineage. She was the granddaughter of Nahor, Abraham's brother (Gen. 24:15). The writer tells us that she was very good in appearance and an unmarried virgin. Certainly, Abraham's servant saw her outward appearance, but he watched closely to see what her character was like. Only after that was proven to be outstanding does he lavish on her gifts and ask for a place to stay. Rebekah immediately ran to her mother's house to share the news.

Rebecca Meets Isaac by the Way
by James Tissot

Despite the servant's determination to quickly return to Abraham with Isaac's bride-to-be, Rebekah had the freedom to make the decision when to leave. What an enormous decision, too! She did not know much about what she was going into except for Abraham's reputation, his family's origins in her country, and their wealth. She would be leaving all she had ever known behind without having a long time to say goodbye. When asked whether she would leave with Abraham's servant, she answered simply but decisively, "I will go" (Gen. 24:58). Before she left, her family sent her away with a blessing of abundant descendants and security. (God gave a similar blessing to Abraham in Genesis 22:17).

Like the patriarch Abraham decades earlier, our "matriarch in the making" left her homeland to travel to a land of promise

(Gen. 12:1–4). The long and arduous journey she took to the Negev is not described in the Bible but is noticeable on a map. Traveling between the richly resourced lands of Mesopotamia to the southern dry lands of the Negev was over five hundred miles (800 km) and would have taken weeks to cover. What did Rebekah and her female attendant discuss on the way? Did Rebekah talk with Abraham's servant about her future husband? How did Rebekah react to the change of scenery and to her new challenging landscape? Many details are not given, but we are told that one evening Isaac was in a field and he looked up and saw the approaching caravan, just as Rebekah looked up to see Isaac. They were married and Isaac took Rebekah into the tent of his mother Sarah, the biblical writer's way of indicating that Rebekah had stepped into the matriarchal role vacant since Sarah's death.

Family Dynamics

Rebekah describes herself as the "daughter of Bethuel" (Gen. 24:24), but her father fades into the background of the story. He may have been sick or aged, and thus unable to take on the role of the family patriarch. The narrative says that Rebekah ran to her "mother's household," not her father's (verse 28). Laban and Bethuel are mentioned, but Laban's name is listed first suggesting Laban was the one making decisions (verse 50). When the servant wanted to return to Abraham, Rebekah's brother and her mother protested and tried to delay his departure (verse 55). These details suggest that Rebekah's father was not present for the marriage negotiations. As the older brother, Laban may have been stepping into the patriarchal role, but Rebekah's mother, as well as Rebekah herself, had input on the marriage.

Our study ends with Rebekah and Isaac beginning a life together, but their story in the Bible is not over. For twenty years, they did not have children. When Rebekah finally got pregnant, God told her the younger twin boy, Jacob, was the descendant God would use to turn their family into a nation. Rebekah favored her younger son and helped him receive the blessing of the firstborn. Her actions can be interpreted in many ways, but Rebekah remained a decisive woman throughout her whole life. Though Scripture doesn't record her death, we're told later in Genesis that Rebekah was buried in the promised land alongside Abraham, Sarah, and Isaac (Gen. 49:31).

Rebekah's Journey to the Negev

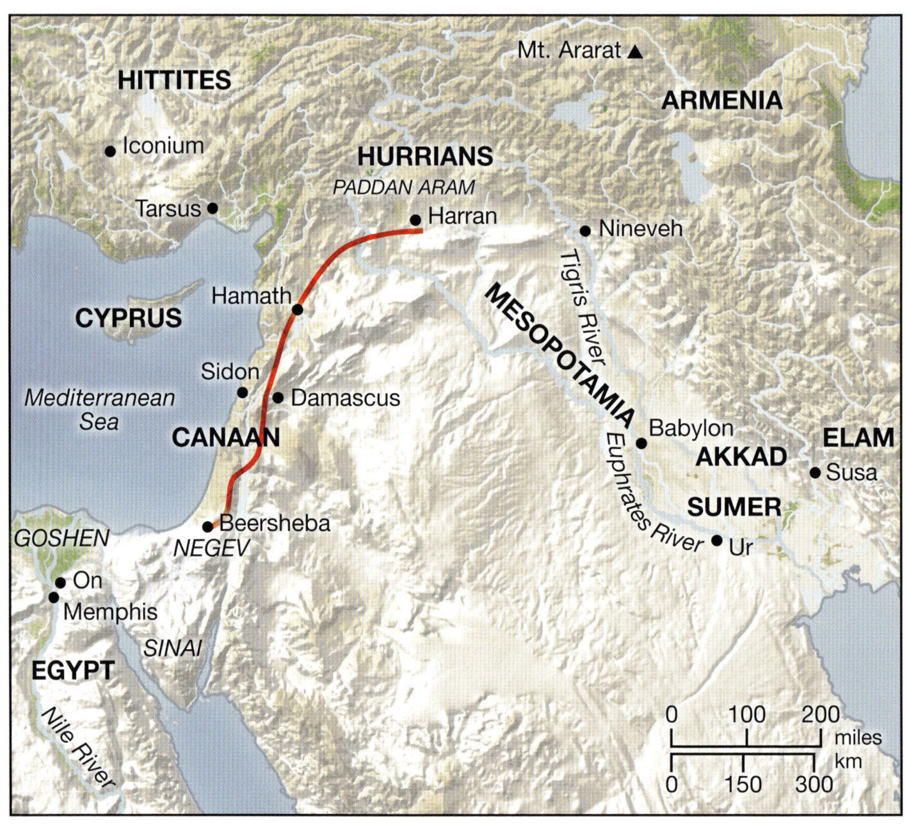

(Exact starting location in Mesopotamia is unknown.)

Live It

In this narrative, Rebekah was a matriarch in the making. When choosing a wife for Isaac, Abraham's servant looked for a woman who had depth of character, and Rebekah's shined through. The servant noticed her instincts for hard work, generosity, and hospitality before inviting her to step into the role of the young matriarch in Abraham's family.

Life Application Questions

1. What do you think motivates Rebekah's actions in this story? (You might find different motives for different actions.)

2. How do Rebekah's words and actions reveal her character? Reflect on how others would describe your character by looking at your words and actions.

3. Do you have women in your life who hold the role of matriarch in your family, church, or community? What, if any, characteristics do they share with Rebekah?

4. Rebekah gave up so much to be the matriarch in the family God chose to use for the redemption of the world, and she did so without knowing the full story. Can you think of a time when you followed God's calling for you without knowing the full story?

5. Rebekah was decisive throughout her life, but making big decisions often doesn't come easy for most of us. What decisions are you wrestling with right now?

Prayer

God of Sarah, Rebekah, and Rachel

God of mothers and those who long to be mothers.

God of the outspoken and the silenced.

God of those who plead, wait, and struggle.

Remember your daughters today.

Remember those who long for love

Remember your promises to those who carry your image in the world.

Remember those to whom you gave a message to share and a part to play in your story.

Remember those to whom you gave a voice and sense of purpose.

(Closing prayers in this study are adapted from Rachel Asproth's "A Prayer for Women: Remember Your Daughters." Used by permission.)

2 THE FIVE SISTERS

Sisters Who Shaped the Law

The Five Sisters

The Old Testament book of Numbers could almost be called the book of *names*. It's not only packed with numbers and narratives about the Israelites in the wilderness, but also with a host of names—and nearly all refer to men. So in chapter 27, when we are introduced to five sisters by name—Mahlah, Noah, Hoglah, Milkah, and Tirzah—we immediately know that we should sit up a little straighter and pay close attention to what is about to happen. Why? Because mentioning women in a genealogy like this was rare, especially five from the same generation.

The sisters' father was from the generation that came out of slavery in Egypt in the exodus and became the Israelite nation. But that young nation of newly-freed slaves had difficulty trusting in God's provision and strength.

When we meet up with the five sisters in the book of Numbers, the Israelites are about to enter the promised land. A census had been taken which would largely determine who would be allotted portions of the land. At a time when only men were counted in censuses and inherited land, these five unmarried sisters, who had no living father or brothers, were left in a very precarious situation.

Key Bible Passage

For this session, read Numbers 27:1–11; 36:1–13.

Optional Reading

The census: Numbers 26:1–4, 52–56, 63–65 (This passage explains how the land was divided and how the original generation died in the wilderness and are not counted for those who inherit land.)

Allotment of the land: Joshua 17:1–6

"What Zelophehad's daughters are saying is right. You must certainly give them property."

NUMBERS 27:7

Know It

1. This narrative lists the women's names nearly every time they are referred to. Why might the biblical writer have chosen to do so? How might the story seem different if they were only identified in reference to their father—"the daughters of Zelophehad"?

2. Who was in the audience as the five sisters stated their request? Notice the attitude with which they approach Moses. How would you describe it?

3. What are your first impressions of the people in this story—the women, Moses, the clan leaders?

Explore It

Culture

During this time in Israelite history, people's identities were organized according to tribes (as opposed to a nation organized under a king). You may notice from genealogies in the Bible that people were in families, and families formed clans, and clans formed tribes. The elders of the tribes held the highest leadership roles among the people, outside of Moses or the priests.

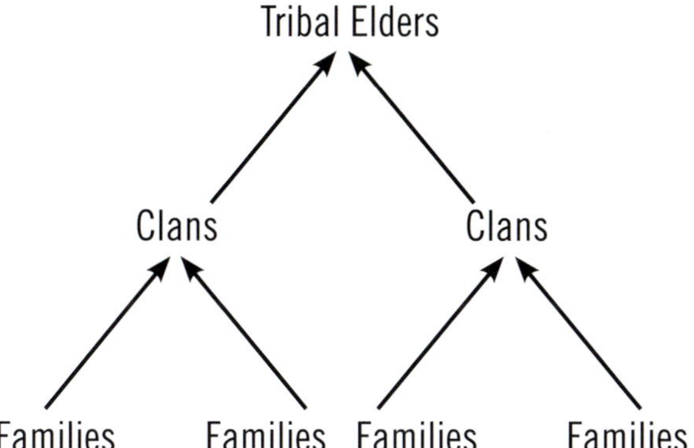

This type of social structure highly valued loyalty and family honor. People prioritized actions and made decisions based on relationships and networks. The family and the community were valued more than the individual. Children were taught to avoid shame and to maintain honor for the sake of the reputation of the whole family.

Each tribe was organized around a *patriarchal* and *patrilocal* structure, but there was also a *patrilineal* element. This meant that family inheritance was passed down through the sons. This practice was supported by the patrilocal aspect of life in which a woman left her home to go to her husband's household. Family land remained with male children, and for the ancient Israelite people, their wealth was contained in their land and in their flocks. Physical property was passed from generation to generation along with knowledge about the viability of the soil, fruitfulness of the plants, and the productivity of the sheep and goats. For a family's future to be sustained through each generation, the wealth needed to be kept in one place. Although the inheritance was distributed among the boys, it stayed in the family. If the land was given to women who departed to live with a different family when they married, who would take care of the land? These issues play a large unspoken role in the story of the five sisters.

Patriarchal: A family organized around the authority and privilege of the oldest living male.

Patrilocal: A concept of living space centered around the male members of the family. The woman moves into her husband's house after marriage.

Patrilineal: Tracing family lineage exclusively through males in the family.

Geography

This story takes place on the plains of Moab, an easy detail to miss because it doesn't seem to contribute to the story of the five sisters. But this detail tells us something important. The Israelites were at the end of their forty years of wandering in the wilderness, camped on the flat plains of Moab on the eastern side of the Jordan River north of the Dead Sea. From here, they could gaze across the valley and see the land God promised to give to them. They were so close to their goal!

Think about the built up expectation for this time. The previous generation of Israelites were slaves in Egypt. They were the ones who stood at the base of Mount Sinai when God made a covenant with his people. That generation had children while they roamed through the vast expanse of the dry wilderness lands. They would have told their children stories of the oppression in Egypt and

View from Mount Nebo near the biblical plains of Moab, facing west overlooking the Dead Sea

God's promise to give them a land of their own. We do not know how old the daughters of Zelophehad were as they stood on the plains of Moab, but we know they had never experienced what it was like to belong to a place and to have land to farm. The simple detail that they were on the plains of Moab means they knew this was the end of the journey, but they also knew they would not inherit property in the new land unless they were bold enough to ask Moses for it.

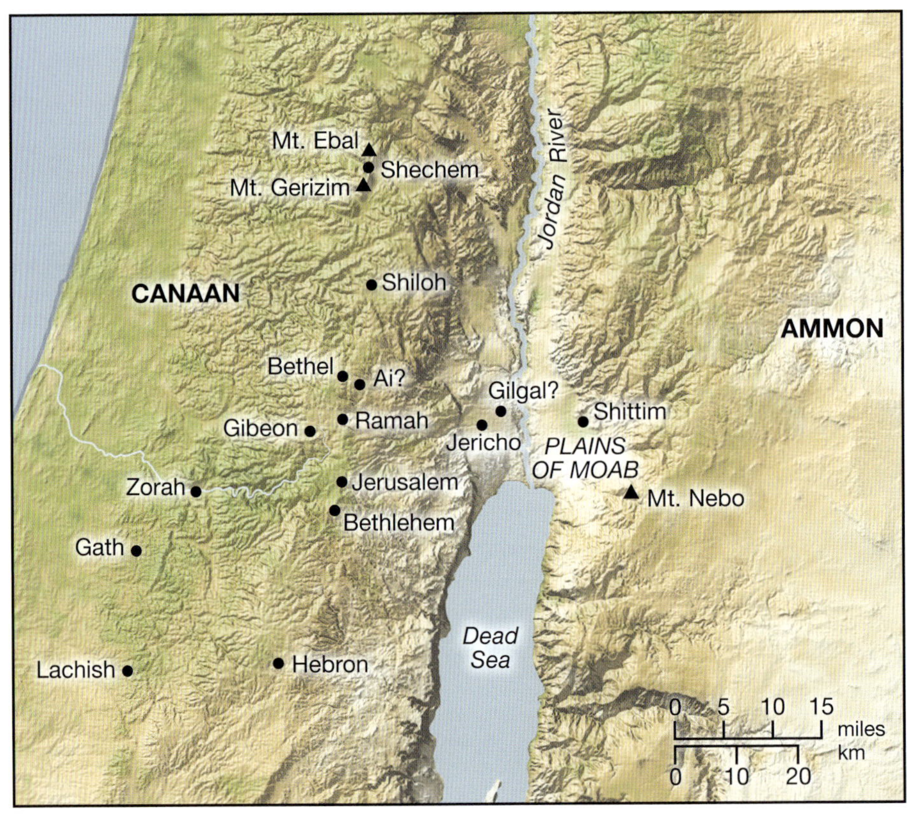

Narrative

The Israelites were in the wilderness for several decades due to their fear and disobedience to God. The original generation of Israelites who left Egypt were dying, and the next generation would enter the land God promised to give to them as an inheritance.

To facilitate the planning process, God told Moses and Eleazar, son of Aaron, to conduct a census (Num. 26:1–4), and the land would be allotted to the people accordingly. Naturally, within the patriarchal system, the heads of the household were counted. You may already notice a problem with the plan. If a family did not have a male leader, then no one was counted in the census. If the family was not counted, then they would not receive a portion of the inheritance God promised his people.

Who noticed the problem? Those who were directly affected by the gap in the inheritance law and who had the family honor to protect—the family with no male heir to defend or preserve the family name.

The daughters of Zelophehad stepped forward to make their case before Moses, Eleazar, the leaders, and the whole assembly. Before the tent of meeting—and therefore before God—they publicly stated that their father had died but that his death should not prevent his name from disappearing among the clan. Without sons, who would inherit land and pass on their father's name to the next generation? The women claimed that they should be given the inheritance.

Presenting their argument took courage. They stood before the top leaders of their community and made their case themselves, challenging the cultural assumptions of their day. Their request was not selfish but a practical one to preserve the honor and name of their family.

Remarkably, we do not see their mother in the story. Was she alive? How had she influenced her daughters? Was she in the background helping them establish their case before Moses? We also do not see the reaction from the crowd. Did they scoff at the request? Were they incredulous at the women's boldness, or perhaps their faith was bolstered by the sisters' stubborn faith in God's promises?

Moses brought their case before God, and God affirmed the rightness of the claim. The daughters should certainly be given their father's share of the land. But the ruling was not only for the daughters of Zelophehad. God told Moses that any male with no son should give an inheritance to his daughters, and only if he had no daughters should the inheritance go to his brothers or to his uncles. Take a moment to think about how that ruling took people who were vulnerable because of the structure of society and gave them a sense that they could take action and be empowered.

The Tribe of Manasseh

The five sisters were the daughters of Zelophehad, who was the son of Hepher, who was a descendant of Gilead in the tribe of Manasseh, one of the largest tribes of Israel. But their ancestor, Manasseh, was not one of the twelve sons of Jacob from whom we get the other tribal names. So who was Manasseh?

When Joseph, one of Jacob's favorite sons, ended up in a position of great power in Egypt, Pharaoh arranged for Joseph to marry Asenath, the daughter of Potiphera, a priest of On (Gen. 41:45). Joseph and Asenath, his Egyptian wife, had two children, Ephraim and Manasseh, who inherited from Jacob as if they were Jacob's own sons (Gen. 48). So two of the largest tribes in the Israelite nation, the tribes of Manasseh and Ephraim, were from the half-Egyptian sons of Joseph.

The sisters' request was a remarkable one. Embedded in it was evidence of their faith in God that they would enter the land God promised to give to the Israelites. These women were proof that the next generation was different from the former generation. Where one generation failed, the next generation would succeed.

Numbers 36 presents an epilogue to the story. The leaders of the tribe of Manasseh sought clarification about this new change in the law. When a woman who inherited land married and relocated to her husband's house, who would work her land? The land could not be left derelict, and the tribe certainly did not want to lose the land. Moses granted the elders' request that the daughters of Zelophehad be required to marry within the tribe. The ruling suggests that even if the daughters married and had children, the children would inherit the property belonging to Zelophehad and thus his memory and his name would be preserved within the tribe.

The Sisters' Names

NAME	MEANING IN HEBREW
Mahlah	possibly "infirmed" or "weak one"
Noah	"rest" or "comfort"
Hoglah	"partridge"
Milkah	"queen"
Tirzah	"pleasant one" or "compensation"

The narrative in Numbers in not the last time we see the sisters. They appear again in Joshua 17. Their faith had paid off, and they had entered the land of promise. When it came time to divvy out the land to the tribes, the sisters stood before Joshua to remind him of the promise they received from Moses in the wilderness. They too were given land.

Although there are no more stories about the five sisters, we do see possible traces of their influence in Manasseh's territory. Among the ruins of Samaria, archaeologists found written records on broken pieces of pottery. In the records, two names that were either cities or tribal subdivisions were Noah and Hoglah. From biblical history we know that one of the capital cities in the northern kingdom was called Tirzah (1 Kings 15:33). Perhaps in these names, we see the memory of these women and their influence preserved for future generations.

Time Line

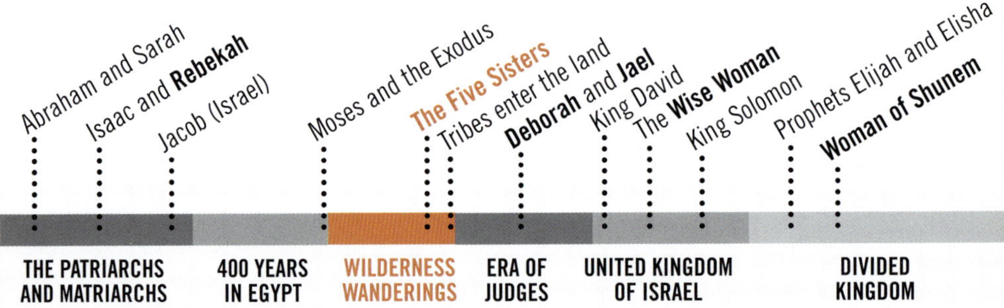

Live It

These five sisters made a precedent-setting request before they even saw the land of inheritance. Their boldness and pursuit of justice resulted in a changed law that influenced women in future generations. They did not have what we'd assume to be the proper social credibility to influence the law, and yet they courageously stood before God, Moses, and the people to reveal a gap in the law and ask for it to be set right. The Bible honors them as women who sought justice.

Today women are in the court system as lawyers and judges in the pursuit of justice. But the courts are not the only place where justice must be pursued. We need to look to our neighborhoods, work environment, urban settings, and, yes, the church.

Life Application Questions

1. What does this story teach us about how God uses people to further his greater story for humankind—and about God's character?

2. These women had the courage to believe that God's promises were for them too. Which of God's promises do you struggle to believe apply to you? (Explore some of the reasons that might be. Engage in a conversation about this both with God and friends who know you well, and listen for any insights you might receive.)

3. Think of a time when you wanted to stand up for yourself or others. If you did so, what did that look like, and what was required of you? If you didn't, what kept you from doing so?

4. Historically, women played a significant role in the Abolitionist (anti-slavery) and Suffragist (women's right to vote) movements. Who is a woman—either from history or someone you know—that you admire for her relentless pursuit of justice?

5. What actions can you take to contribute to a just society for the next generation?

Prayer

God of Mahlah, Noah, Hoglah, Milkah, and Tirzah,

God of the seekers of justice and righteousness,

God of the widow and the orphan,

God of the oppressed and forgotten,

Remember your daughters today.

Remember those who are not seen by those who make decisions.

Remember those to whom you gave a voice to speak your truth.

Remember those who restore justice in their communities.

Remember us who are your daughters of your inheritance.

3

DEBORAH & JAEL

Courageous Judge and Feisty Warrior

Deborah & Jael

Deborah and Jael lived in a time period after the Israelites entered the land of inheritance under Joshua's leadership, but before Israel had a king to rule over and unite the tribes. People were loyal to their families, clans, and tribes, but the bond between the tribes was fraying quickly.

The book of Judges, where we find the stories of Deborah and Jael, records the downward spiral of Israelite society, as the people fell away from God's design for life and instead did whatever they thought was right in their own eyes. Yet God pursued his wayward people. He raised up a series of leaders, called judges, to remind the people of his power and love for them.

This time period in the history of Israel has been called the era of the judges, and one of those early judges was a woman named Deborah.

Read It

Key Bible Passage

For this session, read Judges 2:10–19; 4:1–24.

Optional Reading

The victory song of Deborah: Judges 5:1–31

"The LORD will deliver Sisera into the hands of a woman."

JUDGES 4:9

Know It

1. Judges 2:10–19 gives the reader a pattern that is repeated throughout the book of Judges. Write down each step of the cycle from this passage that begins with a new Israelite generation and concludes with the death of the judge.

2. From the story in Judges 4, how would you describe Deborah's and Jael's characters and actions? What words come to mind?

3. Deborah and Jael were both strong women whose actions impacted Israel, but they lived in different spheres of influence—an Israelite judge and prophet, and a Canaanite tent-dweller. How might their lives have been different from one another?

Geography

The land God gave to the Israelites features a large mountain range stretching north-south through the middle. This geography forced the international trade—and with it wealth, armies, and large cities—to orient north and south on the flatter, easier-to-traverse ground on the eastern or western side of the mountain range.

One of the only gaps through the mountain range is the Jezreel Valley. This valley looks like a broken triangle that points toward the Mediterranean Sea. The valley is wide and almost table-top flat, which invited even the laziest of travelers to pass through. Its shape is outlined by the surrounding hills. Runoff water from those hills pulls soil into the valley, which results in a thick, rich agricultural bed. The singular Kishon River drains water out of the fertile valley. Given the flatness of the terrain, one rainstorm could bog down any ancient traveler as the thick bed of soil quickly turned into mud.

In Old Testament times, local and international powers fought to control this valuable land. Its importance is reflected in the dozens of biblical stories that happened here, including the battle in Judges 4.

A view over the Jezreel Valley to Mount Tabor (photo by Cyndi Parker)

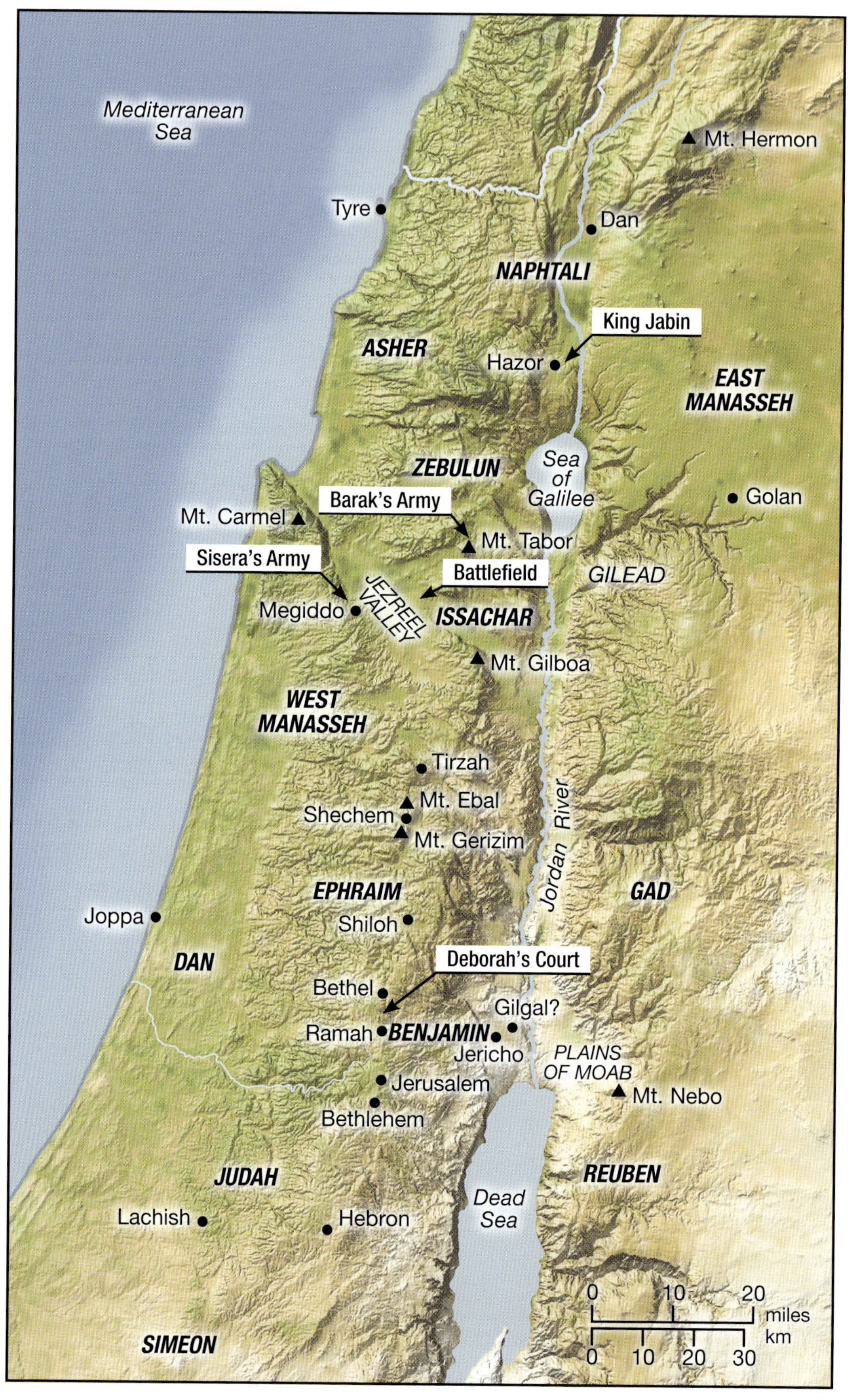

Mediterranean Sea
Mt. Hermon
Tyre
Dan
NAPHTALI
King Jabin
ASHER
Hazor
EAST MANASSEH
ZEBULUN
Sea of Galilee
Golan
Mt. Carmel
Barak's Army
Mt. Tabor
Sisera's Army
Battlefield
GILEAD
JEZREEL VALLEY
Megiddo
ISSACHAR
Mt. Gilboa
WEST MANASSEH
Tirzah
Mt. Ebal
Shechem
Mt. Gerizim
Jordan River
EPHRAIM
GAD
Joppa
Shiloh
DAN
Deborah's Court
Bethel
Gilgal?
Ramah
BENJAMIN
Jericho
PLAINS OF MOAB
Jerusalem
Mt. Nebo
Bethlehem
JUDAH
REUBEN
Dead Sea
Lachish
Hebron
SIMEON
0 10 20 miles
0 10 20 30 km

Time Line

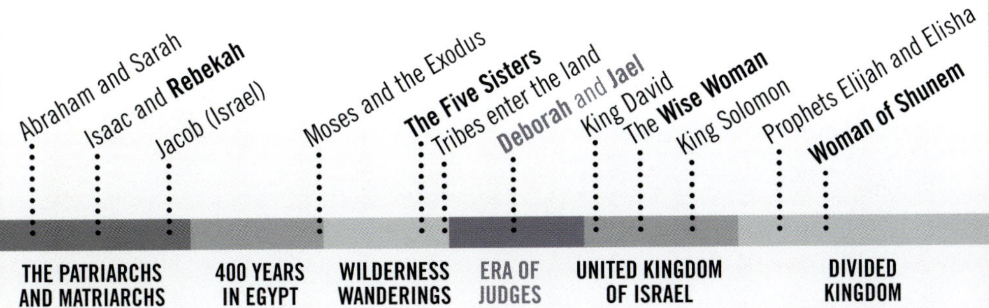

Narrative

Deborah instructed Barak to gather an army and go to Mount Tabor on the northeastern corner of the Jezreel Valley, where God would join him in battle against Sisera. King Jabin and his general Sisera had "cruelly oppressed the Israelites for twenty years" with their army, nine hundred chariots strong (Judg. 4:3). Some interpreters scorn Barak for agreeing to go only if Deborah went with him, but it's more likely that his request was not a sign of weakness as much as it was a display of confidence in Deborah and his willingness to follow the one who spoke the words of God.

The scene for the battle was set in the wide open plain of the Jezreel Valley. Sisera was stationed at Megiddo along the southern edge of the valley. His job as the general for Jabin, king of Hazor, was to maintain control over the trade routes and wealth flowing through the valley. When he was told that the Israelites had gathered for battle behind Mount Tabor, he summoned his men and his nine hundred chariots. The scene is almost laughable. The Israelites were farmers turned foot soldiers when required, and they were going up against an army with iron chariots!

Despite the mismatched armies, Deborah instructed Barak to charge into battle: "Go! This is the day the Lord has given Sisera into your hands. Has not the Lord gone ahead of you?"

(Judg. 4:14). She displayed tremendous trust in God's victory before the battle even started.

Judges 4 says that God routed Sisera and all his chariots, and Sisera fled his own chariot on foot (verse 15). The next chapter in Judges, known as the "Song of Deborah," is a more poetic and dramatic retelling of the battle:

> *From the heavens the stars fought,*
> *from their courses they fought against Sisera.*
> *The river Kishon swept them away.*
> *(Judg. 5:20–21)*

What do you think it means for the heavens to fight against Sisera and the river to sweep the army away? A huge thunderstorm hit the valley! The flat Jezreel Valley—normally conducive for chariot activity, and thus giving Sisera the upper hand—was turned into a valley filled with mud. That which had been Sisera's strength became his weakness. His army was routed, and he was forced to flee on foot.

But the battle was not over. The story now moves from the public arena of a battlefield to a personal level and into the private sphere of a tent. Jael was a non-Israelite, part of a semi-nomadic clan called the Kenites. Among such clans, women were the ones who set up the heavy, goat-haired tents. A hammer and a tent peg were common tools that felt comfortable in Jael's hands.

Jael was standing at the opening of her tent when she saw Sisera approach. Was she outside because the sounds of the battle captured her attention? Was she wary of a rogue soldier coming near her tent? We do not know if she had family or children to protect. When we read the words of Sisera's mother when he failed to return home, we see the potential danger Jael is in. In Judges 5:28–30, Sisera's mother hopes his lateness returning was because he was busy with the soldiers dividing the spoils of victory, which included "a woman or two for each man." The horrific imagery is compounded by the fact that Sisera's mother was not bothered by the idea of her son raping foreign women, and she goes on to hope that Sisera will bring back their stolen garments to adorn her own neck!

We hold our breath as Jael extends a dangerous invitation for Sisera to enter her tent. Her hospitality was disarming. Sisera asked her for water but she gave him milk. Then she covered him with a blanket. Pause and imagine the scene; a woman in a tent, giving someone milk and covering him with a blanket. What does it make you think of? If you say a mom nursing a baby, that is probably close to what the biblical writer wants you to think of, because the next sentence continues the thought. Sisera says, "If someone comes by and asks you, 'Is there a man in there?' say 'No'" (Judg. 4:20). The initially terrifying scene becomes darkly humorous, because we know there is no grown "man" in the tent—only a baby.

Jael Showing Sisera Lying Dead to Barak by James Tissot

The poetic description of Sisera's death at the hands of Jael in Judges 5 is more graphic than in chapter 4. The repetition of words and phrases forces the reader to grapple with Jael's actions. Twice we are told Sisera fell between her feet (Judg. 5:27). The image plays a two-fold purpose. When this scene is coupled with chapter 4 in which Sisera was treated like a baby, chapter 5 seems like a grotesque birthing scene in which Sisera falls in a bloody mess between Jael's feet. Alternatively, the scene can be read as "the punishment fits the crime." Sisera would have been out brutally raping women, but instead he falls dead between Jael's feet.

Before the battle, Deborah had prophesied to Barak that "the LORD will deliver Sisera into the hands of a woman" (Judg. 4:9). Jael executed the final blow to break the yoke of oppression. In the song in Judges 5, Jael is called "most blessed of women" (verse 24). What an amazing statement to make at the end of a narrative about Deborah. This non-Israelite woman, Jael, is held in high regard in the narrative because her actions destroyed the enemy of Israel.

God delivered the Israelites from the oppressive rule of King Jabin, and he did so using a woman in the public sphere and a woman in the private sphere. They both played essential roles in God's plan.

Who Was Deborah?

Deborah's name means "hornet, wasp, wild honey bee" and she is referred to in Judges 4:4, in Hebrew, as *'eshet lappidot,* "the wife of Lapidote." In this description, the word for *wife* can also be translated as "woman of" and *lappidot* as "flames." Many Bible translators choose to describe Deborah as the "wife of Lapidote," because in a patriarchal world women were commonly known as "the wife of ... ." But Deborah can just as easily be called "a woman of flames." This translation works nicely in the story, because Barak, the man who led the army in battle, has a name that means "lightning." The "woman of flames" and "lightning" go into battle together.

We are introduced to Deborah as a prophet and a judge who was stationed in the heart of the Israelite hill country between the cities of Ramah and Bethel. Her role in Israel was to interpret the law and help settle disputes (Judg. 4:5; see also Deut. 16:18–20). Does this surprise you? It can be easy to assume that only men could hold these roles in ancient Israel. Yet, as we saw in the last session with the five sisters, there is nothing about gender that prevented anyone from interpreting the law. The Old Testament also mentions several female prophets, such as Miriam (Ex. 15:20), Huldah (2 Kings 22:14), and Isaiah's wife (Isa. 8:3). Deborah was in an acceptable and rightful position of influence as a prophet and judge, and God chose her to lead the people out of twenty long years of oppression.

When we shy away from reading Old Testament stories with battle scenes and violence, we miss out on stories of women like Deborah and Jael. These stories are uncomfortable to read, because they portray complex and sometimes horrific aspects of life, and yet God remains present in them.

Like modern women, Deborah and Jael could not choose their gender, their time period, or their social context. These kinds of stories show us that God is not only present within times of peace, but also times of war.

God routinely breaks assumptions about who he can use to carry out his purposes. In this story, God came to the aid of his people through men and women, Israelites and non-Israelites, a leader of the country and a common tent-dweller. In the end, Deborah's leadership in wartime led to peace for forty years, which was one of the longest times of peace recorded in Judges. Jael's courage to kill Sisera destroyed Israel's enemy and made her remembered through history as most blessed among women.

Life Application Questions

1. Which characters (if any) in this story do you identify with the most? Why?

2. What feelings come up for you as you consider some of the graphic imagery in this story (killing, birthing, plunder, rape)? How can grappling with Old Testament narratives like this help us understand the greater message of Scripture?

3. What do you think about the biblical writer calling Jael the "most blessed of women"? When, if ever, do you believe violence is justified?

4. What does this story tell us about vulnerability and power—not just then, but also now?

5. In your own words, describe the faith exhibited by Deborah. How can that type of faith be expressed in your life?

Prayer

God of Deborah and Jael,

God of public defenders and private leaders,

God of the soldier and of the peacemaker

God of men and of women,

Remember your daughters today.

Remember those forced into war to protect their families.

Remember the ones who walk with confidence of your provision.

Remember those who experience unjust violence from a cruel world.

Remember those who need your healing balm and comforting touch.

Notes

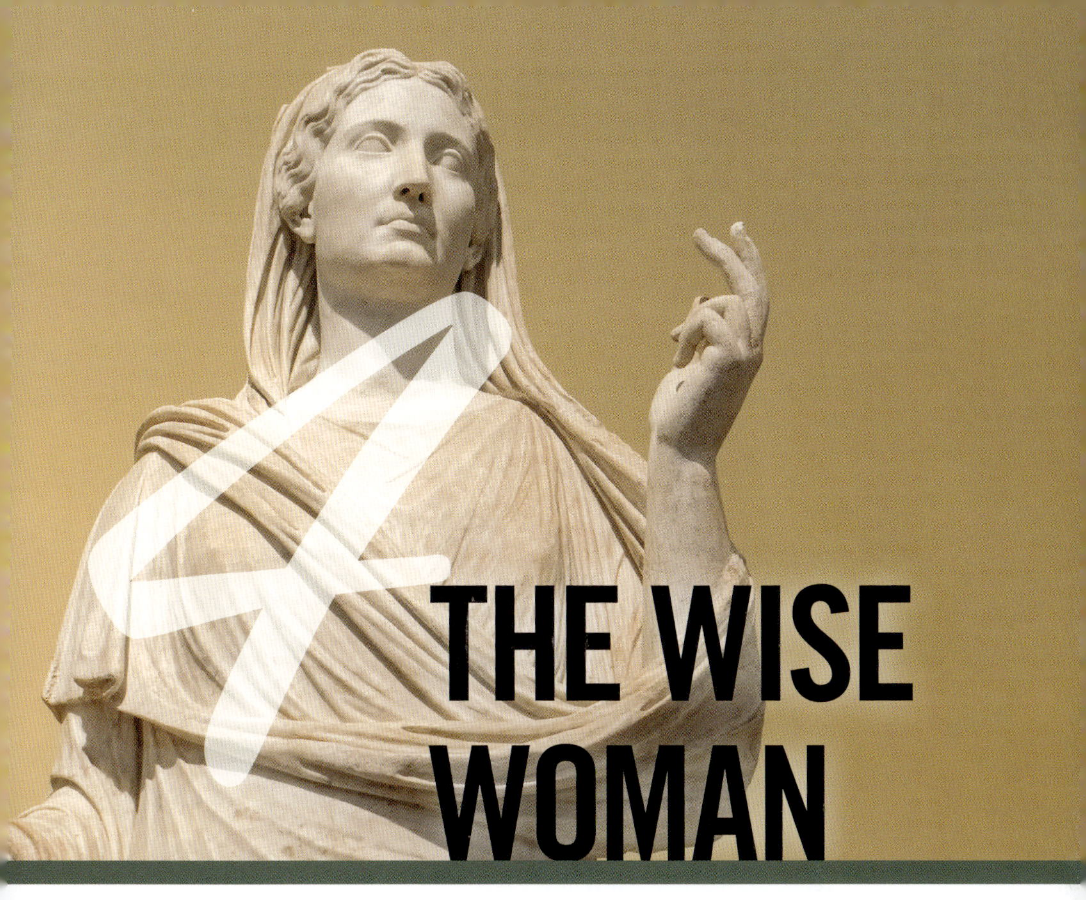

A Bold Negotiator

The Wise Woman

She is an Old Testament hero you may have never heard of. Her story, only nine verses long in the Bible, is rarely retold in Christian communities today. Though history did not preserve her name, she is known in the Bible as the wise woman of the city of Abel Beth Maakah.

In the scope of the story of Israel in the Old Testament, she played a small role, yet for the people of her city she was a savior. She diplomatically challenged perpetrators of violence and prevented bloodshed.

As you work through this study, think about what characteristics make her wise, and how God used her in her community. Consider also what we today gain by reading, studying, and teaching the story of this wise woman from long ago, instead of skipping over those handful of verses.

Read It

Key Bible Passage

For this session, read 2 Samuel 20:14–22.

Optional Reading

Joab's pursuit of Sheba: 2 Samuel 20:1–13

The wise woman of Tekoa: 2 Samuel 14:1–20

> "While they were battering the wall to bring it down, a wise woman called from the city, 'Listen! Listen!'"
>
> 2 SAMUEL 20:15–16

Know It

1. Who are the important characters in this story? How are they each portrayed? (Read 2 Samuel 20:1–2 for more information about Sheba.)

2. How does Sheba's silence in the narrative affect those around him? How does the voice of the wise woman affect those around her?

3. What does this story reveal about the roles women had in Israelite society in Old Testament times?

Culture

After the era of the judges, the Israelite tribes were united under a single king, but they also maintained a local governing structure. Respected elders who lived admirable lives held authority as local judges. They were educated in God's laws and settled disputes (see Ex. 18:13–23; Deut. 16:18–20). Historically, those legal cases took place at the city gate of a walled city.

A wall around a city was necessary for protection, but it also cut people off from their land where they grew food and fed sheep and goats. Families who lived in walled cities kept their farming equipment and stores of food inside their houses, but they had to leave the city every morning to go into their fields to work. Since members of every family exited and entered through the one opening in the wall, the city gate became a public gathering place of buying and selling goods, begging for money and food, trading news from surrounding villages, and settling disputes before a local judge.

Not every Israelite lived inside the walls of a city. Some families set up small communities in outlying areas. They may have taken extra produce to the larger cities to sell, but when armies marched through their area, the families fled into the protected area of the walled city.

We know the woman in this narrative as the wise woman of Abel Beth Maakah. Many women throughout the Bible act wisely and give wise council, but the woman in this story seems to be known as the *wise woman* in the city. A similar narrative in 2 Samuel 14 also centers around a woman called "the wise woman of Tekoa." Since neither of these women's names are mentioned, it's possible that the designation "wise woman" may be more than a simple description, but rather an official role within the community.

The fact that Abel Beth Maakah had a wall surrounding the city suggests it was of significant size and influence in the area. If "wise woman" was an official title, the woman in our story may have sat at the city gate, helping solve local disputes. As you will see in the narrative, her city had a reputation for caring for outlying villages.

Geography

The action in 2 Samuel 20 begins near the capital city of Jerusalem. King David, who had united the tribes of Israel and established the kingdom of Israel, just experienced a near fatal blow to his reign when his son Absalom staged a coup. At the conclusion of the failed attempt to replace David, a small insurrectionist group under the leadership of Sheba remained. David believed that he could not afford to ignore Sheba and his men. So he sent Joab, the leader of Israel's army, after Sheba.

Sheba escaped to the far northern reaches of Israel and inside the walls of Abel Beth Maakah. We do not know exactly where Sheba was located when he decided to flee from David's army. However, we do know that David's army left from Jerusalem. The distance from Jerusalem to Abel Beth Maakah was roughly 130 miles (209 km). The biblical writer does not tell us how many days the journey took, but seeing the route on a map helps us imagine the determination Joab and his men must have had. They were on the hunt and on a mission from the king.

Mediterranean Sea
Mt. Hermon
Tyre
Abel Beth Maakah
Dan
Hazor
Sea of Galilee
Golan
Mt. Carmel
Mt. Tabor
GILEAD
JEZREEL VALLEY
Megiddo
Shunem
Mt. Gilboa
Mt. Ebal
Shechem
Mt. Gerizim
Jordan River
Joppa
Shiloh
Bethel
Ramah
Gibeon
Jericho
PHILISTIA
Jerusalem
Mt. Nebo
Bethlehem
Dead Sea
Lachish
Hebron
0 10 20 miles
0 10 20 30 km

View of Tel Abel Beth Maakah looking southeast

Narrative

We are introduced to the wise woman when Sheba's rebellion brought the battle to her city. We know nothing of her private life. How old was she? Did she have a family? Did she belong to a long line of wise women? What we do know is that when hundreds of lives were in danger, she stepped in to challenge the actions of the army.

The people of her city must have been shocked and frightened. Their city was being attacked by their own king's army. Joab and his army built a siege ramp outside the walls and started to batter down the walls. People were sheltering inside. We do not know how long the city was under siege. No one would have been permitted in or out of the city, so their crops went unattended. Now their food for the year was in danger. And yet Sheba, whom the army was pursuing, was holed up in the city. He could have told the people why they were under attack, but he kept quiet. He preserved his life at the expense of everyone in the city.

In contrast, the wise woman stopped the army's drive for vengeful violence. She called out for a chance to addresses the army's leader, Joab, directly. She must have been at a high place on the wall for her shouts to be heard. Joab responded by drawing closer to the wall. He was in a vulnerable place, being close to the wall during a siege where he could easily be struck dead (see Judg. 9:53). Even so, the fact that Joab responded favorably to the woman's request to speak with him was a sign of respect for the role she played in the city. (Joab would not have put himself in danger by talking with her close to the wall if she had not been a prominent resident.)

Like a skilled negotiator, she employed a purposeful approach:

- She began the conversation by imploring Joab to listen, which demonstrated the seriousness of what she was about to say. ("Listen to the words of your servant …")
- She identified herself to Joab as "your servant," a humble and non-combative term.
- Then she pointed to the city's history. Theirs was a place where challenging cases were brought before a judge. They were a revered city, known for faithfully administering God's laws. They were a "mother city" and cared for the villages around them.
- She asked why Joab would want to destroy such a respected city. Getting to the heart of the conflict, she found out exactly what the army was after.

Joab responded that the siege was due to their protection of a man who rebelled against the king. The unspoken assumption was that if the city harbored Sheba, they were supporting Sheba's cause. Joab claimed he was there to protect the honor of the king.

The wise woman came up with a simple and alternative response. Instead of Joab's blood-thirsty campaign, the city's residents would find Sheba, kill him, and toss his head over the wall to Joab. She returned to her people and told them the course of action. She did not need to plead her case or ask for input from others. She presented a clear-cut plan. The decision was executed immediately. Sheba was held responsible for his actions and the city proved it was not willingly harboring the fugitive, nor were they rebelling against King David. The city was safe, and the army returned to Jerusalem.

Time Line

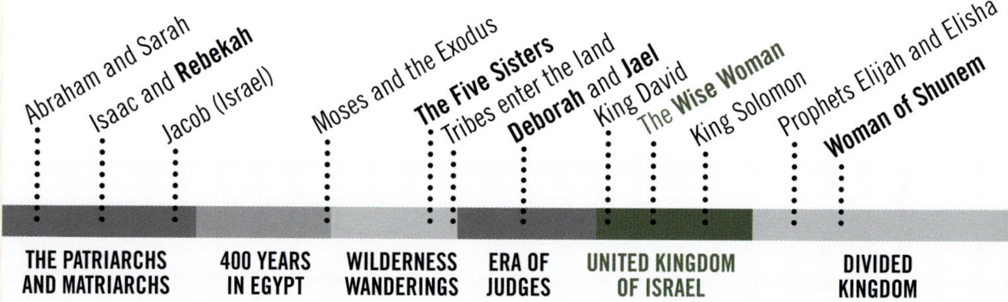

Live it

The story about the wise woman of Abel Beth Maakah gives us an interesting glimpse into Israelite life away from the royal palace or the temple in Jerusalem. There are hints about how larger cities acted as protectors for the nearby villages. We notice a community that respected a woman's wisdom and leadership enough to place her in a position of authority. We see an army on the rampage and a woman bold enough to confront unnecessary violence and save her community.

Life Application Questions

1. What piqued your curiosity or surprised you when you read this story? Why did that stand out to you?

2. In the wise woman's boldness, where does she show wisdom? How do her actions change the direction of the story?

3. What type of leadership qualities do you notice in the wise woman? How do you see those qualities reflected in your own life or in the lives of other women you know?

4. Do you consider courage as an aspect of wisdom? How or why not?

5. Read these wise sayings from Proverbs, the book of wisdom:

- Proverbs 15:1
- Proverbs 16:32
- Proverbs 25:15
- Proverbs 28:1

What wise advice have you received—or offered to someone—when facing a crisis or navigating a conflict?

Prayer

God of the wise women among us.

God of the defenders of the weak.

God of the courageous who speak on behalf of others.

God of those who feel vulnerable in their communities.

Remember your daughters today.

Remember those to whom you gave the gift of leadership.

Remember the women who suffer from violence.

Remember those who are mothers to people around them even when they are not her physical children.

Remember the women who take risks to save the less fortunate.

5 THE WOMAN OF SHUNEM

A Woman of Hospitality

The Woman of Shunem

After the death of King Solomon, the kingdom of Israel fell into a brutal civil war which resulted in the kingdom splitting in two—into a northern kingdom and a southern one.

The books of 1 and 2 Kings (as their names suggest) record the exploits of dozens of northern and southern kings. But scattered throughout these epic narratives are the stories of common men and women struggling to survive. In their stories, we get a break from the drama of national events and are allowed to peek into the lives of ordinary individuals—such as the woman from the village of Shunem who we'll focus on in this session.

These minor characters may not contribute much to the larger national drama of ancient Israel; yet their stories are important enough to be preserved in God's Word. *Why are they here? Why does God want us to read and remember their stories?* As you work through this session's narrative, stay curious about what the story of the woman of Shunem can tell you about God's character.

Key Bible Passage

For this session, read 2 Kings 4:8–37.

Optional Reading

The Shunammite woman's land restored: 2 Kings 8:1–6.

> "She saddled the donkey and said to her servant, 'Lead on; don't slow down.' ... So she set out and came to the man of God at Mount Carmel."
>
> 2 KINGS 4:24–25

Know It

1. Notice how many times Elisha tried to communicate with her through his servant Gehazi. How does the woman respond? What does this suggest about her character?

2. What words might you use to describe the woman of Shunem—her attitude and actions?

3. What (if any) similarities do you see between her and other women from this study: Rebekah, the five sisters, Deborah, Jael, and the wise woman?

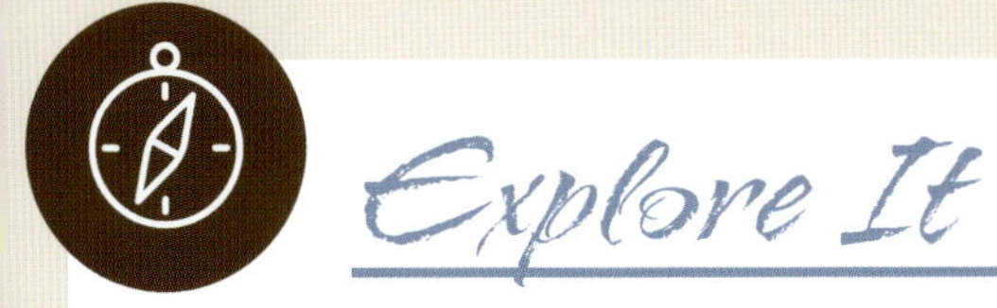

Explore It

Geography

The woman from Shunem lived in a region you have already encountered in this study. In the session about Deborah and Jael, we looked at the importance of the Jezreel Valley. On the far eastern edge of that valley was a long rectangular valley called the Harod Valley. It completed the east-west connection that traders, travelers, and armies envied. The small town of Shunem sat on the northwestern edge of the Harod Valley near the large city of Jezreel, which was where the kings of the northern kingdom of Israel built a palace. At the other end of the valley sat the monumental city of Beth-shan. Shunem was positioned along the heavily traveled international road that skirted to the north of the agriculturally rich fields.

View looking northwest from Jezreel. To the right (east) of center is the Hill of Moreh. The white buildings on its lower left slope mark the site of biblical Shunem. (Photo by www.HolyLandPhotos.org. Used by permission.)

Simply identifying where her hometown was helps us better imagine her world. She lived on desirable land that was rich in agriculture. The international road in the valley would make her accustomed to seeing a variety of travelers from local and foreign places with whom to trade goods and ideas. Shunem may have been a small town, but its location on this significant road and near one of the royal palaces meant that the residents were well informed about political struggles. The woman of Shunem was well placed to notice the prophet Elisha's travels and provide him with hospitality.

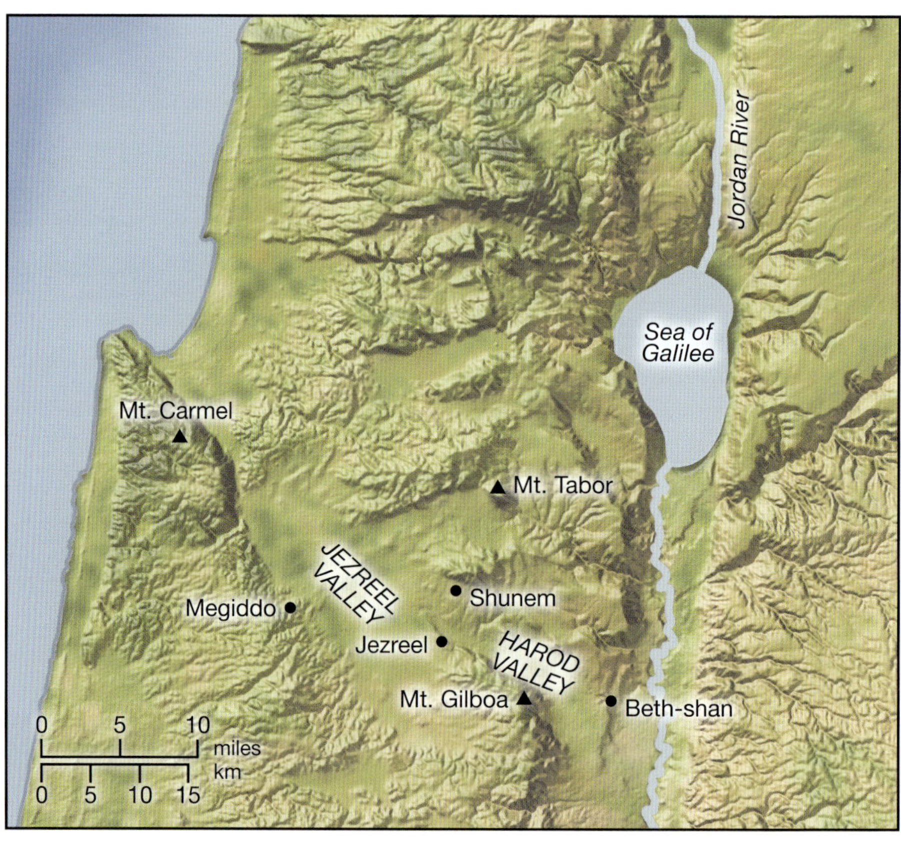

Culture

Hospitality was an essential part of ancient culture, particularly since there were no inns or hotels for travelers. People relied on a host family at each stop to provide food, water, and protection. For any village, hospitality was a form of diplomacy and networking. A traveler received food and protection, while the host not only made sure the traveler was not a threat to the village, but also that the traveler had opportunities to create broader networks of relationships and trade.

Recognizing that Elisha was a man of God who performed miracles, the woman of Shunem opened her home and extended hospitality to him when he traveled through the Harod Valley. By opening her home to Elisha, she opened her home to all who traveled with him. As their relationship grew, the woman's generosity expanded from offering meals to converting part of her house into a room set aside for Elisha. By modern standards, Israelite homes were not large. Every room had multiple purposes. Even the flat roofs during the hot, arid months were used to dry newly harvested grains during the day and then became valuable places to rest when the evening breeze came. The fact that the woman of Shunem not only built and furnished a room but also set it aside as Elisha's room indicates that she was wealthy and also very generous with what she had.

Time Line

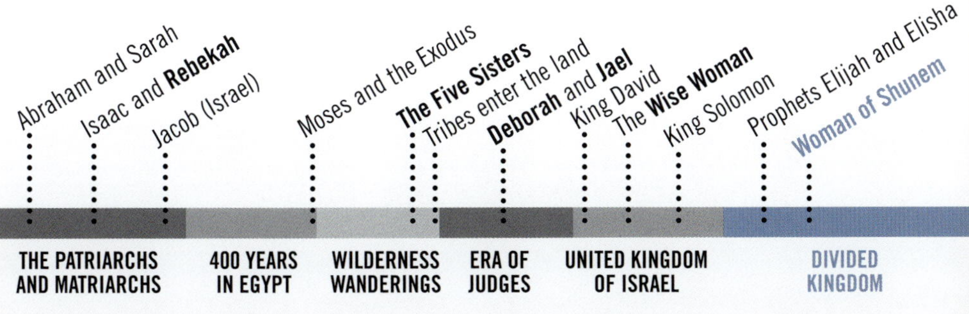

Narrative

Curiously, in an area that would have been busy with trade, travel, and agriculture, few characters are highlighted in this story. The woman's husband is present but in the background. Servants appear for a short time but then fade away. What should be a bustling household is silenced so we can focus on the characters who are present.

At some point, Elisha became motivated to give the woman of Shunem a gift in return for her hospitality. Do you notice what is unusual about the sequence of events in 2 Kings 4:12–17? Elisha offered to speak to the king or to men of great authority on the woman's behalf, but she dismissed his offer. Either she was confident that her community would always support her or she was taking a humble posture and stating she did not require anything of the court. Her generosity was genuine; she neither required nor expected anything in return for her hospitality.

Elisha's servant, Gehazi, then drew Elisha's attention to the woman's social situation. Her husband was old and she had no children. You can hear the patriarchal and patrilineal assumptions in Gehazi's comment (see session one in this study). That situation was not something Elisha could take to the king. Only God could do something miraculous like provide a child. Elisha prophesied that within a year the woman would hold a son in her arms.

Although the woman was content with life among her people, and although she did not ask Elisha for a child, there seems to be a bit of longing and incredulity in her response to Elisha. She did not want such a promise to raise her hopes if it would not come true.

> *"No, my lord!" she objected. "Please, man of God, don't mislead your servant!" (2 Kings 4:16)*

Here we have a woman who breaks our assumptions about women in ancient Israel. She did not express concerns about money, sons, or land. She said she had a home "among my own people," so maybe she did not live with her husband's clan but among her own. Maybe she was a daughter to a father who had no sons, and so she inherited land, like the five sisters. The Bible does not record many stories of women like this, so it's difficult to know how common her situation was. Yet Elisha's promise for a child seems to touch on a true desire the woman dared not hope for unless it would become a reality.

Elisha Raising the Shunammite's Son by Benjamin West

As Elisha had said, the woman of Shunem did bear a son—an unexpected gift from God that she probably doubted would really happen. After some time passed, her son grew to be old enough to help his father harvest crops. One day while in the field, the son fell ill, and the father sent him home to be with his mother. Shortly after arriving, the boy died.

The next sequence of events is remarkable. The woman sent word to her husband that she needed a donkey and a servant, but she did not tell him that his child had died. She was determined to go immediately to Elisha on Mount Carmel on the southwestern side of the Jezreel Valley, a journey that was between 17 and 25 miles (27–40 km).

The prophet saw her at a distance and sent Gehazi out to inquire about her visit, but she would not be detained by explaining the disaster. She needed to speak directly with Elisha.

> *"Did I ask you for a son, my lord?" she said. "Didn't I tell you, 'Don't raise my hopes'?" (2 Kings 4:28)*

Her unspoken plea in these words was for Elisha to do something. He tried to send Gehazi as a representative in his place, but the woman would not allow that. She only trusted the man of God. She would return to her house only if Elisha went with her.

Gehazi ran ahead to do as Elisha asked and to lay the prophet's staff across the boy's body. Nothing happened. When Elisha arrived at the house, he shut himself in with the boy and prayed for God to restore the child. An odd collection of details are given in the next verses. Elisha stretched himself over the boy's body until it began to get warm. The prophet paced about the room and then repeated his actions. The boy sneezed seven times and then opened his eyes, and Elisha returned the boy to his mother!

The story ends abruptly without answering all our questions. Why didn't Elisha's staff work? How long was Elisha in the room praying for the boy's life? When was the father told of what happened? Did other villagers know? These were details the biblical writer did not think were important. Our curiosity might remain, but the story directs our focus to the shared details. A woman recognized that Elisha was a man of God, and she generously provided food and housing for him. She did not seek repayment for her hospitality. God gave the woman a son, and when the son died, God alone through the work of his prophet raised him from the dead.

When you think of Old Testament stories, which come to mind? The exodus epic? Miraculous military exploits of the kings? Royal court dramas? It might be easy to assume that God only interacted with and cared about the mighty influencers in Israelite society, but with Old Testament stories like the woman of Shunem, we know that's not the case. In these stories, we see God, through the prophets, being concerned for the hopes, joys, fears, and griefs of often-forgotten individuals.

Life Application Questions

1. Nowhere in the narrative do we see the woman and Elisha having theological conversations, nor do we see her pleading directly with God. So where do you see evidence of God in this story?

2. At the beginning of this session, we asked the question: *What can this story teach us about God's character?* How would you answer that question now?

3. The woman of Shunem is a minor character in biblical history, and yet God used her. Who are some "minor characters" in your life? If you stopped to pay attention, what might you learn through their lives—their stories?

4. In what ways do you extend hospitality to others? Are you willing to accept hospitality when others extend it to you?

5. Did you have something (or someone) in your life that was once a gift from God, but now you feel the sadness of its loss? Take time to invite God into that situation. Journal about it and then set it before the Lord in prayer.

Prayer

God of all the women who feel forgotten but whom you know by name.

God of the single, the childless, the married, and the widowed.

God of the wealthy and the poor.

God of those who insist they be heard.

Remember your daughters today.

Remember those who use their provisions to benefit others.

Remember those who are organizers and initiators.

Remember the ones who have experienced the loss of a dear friend or family member.

Remember those who cling to the goodness of your promises.

A Figure of Godly Wisdom

Lady Wisdom

There is something special about *wisdom* being represented in the Bible as a woman. It honors the wisdom that women hold in their community. You know this kind of wisdom; it transforms life in meaningful ways. Such wisdom helps us learn how to set priorities, interact with others, and negotiate troublesome situations.

In our previous sessions, we studied different biblical women who embodied wisdom, and now we look at wisdom herself, personified in the book of Proverbs.

Lady Wisdom, as she is sometimes called, is a reliable companion. She encourages people to stay true to God and warns them of tempting yet foolish desires. She is the ultimate teacher. In a book like Proverbs that aims to help us understand words of insight, receive instruction in wise behavior, and do what is right and just and fair, wisdom is the guide for that transformation (Prov. 1:2–4).

In this session, sit at the feet of Lady Wisdom. Watch her carefully and think about how to be like her in your own life.

Read It

Key Bible Passage

For this session, read Proverbs 9:1–18.

Optional Reading

Lady Wisdom's speech: Proverbs 8:1–36

The woman of valor: Proverbs 31:10–31 (As you read, think of this woman as another figure of wisdom.)

> "Wisdom has built her house;
> she has set up its seven pillars."
>
> PROVERBS 9:1

Know It

1. Focus on the two scenes created for you in this passage: one is in Lady Wisdom's house and the other in Dame Folly's house. How is each described?

2. Imagine yourself hearing Wisdom and Folly call out their different invitations to everyone in the city. What might you find enticing about each invitation?

3. Focus on the middle verses of Proverbs 9 (verses 7–12). Which verse would you pick out as the statement that summarizes what this passage is about?

Explore It

Culture

In Proverbs 9, we are invited into the homes of Lady Wisdom and Dame Folly, so we should ask ourselves what Israelite homes looked like in Old Testament times.

Thankfully, archaeologists have uncovered enough homes to give us a general layout. Israelite houses had a simple square or rectangular shape. One door in the middle of the narrow side of the house connected the living space inside the home with the public space outside. A person would pass through the door and enter a long room with additional rooms on either side, which stored farming equipment or sheep. Since the door opened onto the central room, or courtyard, that was the least private room in the house and was therefore used for public activities. Women from the community gathered there to grind grain and bake bread together. They turned tedious daily jobs into communal activities. A broad room spanned the back of the house where valuable goods were stored. The family slept on the upper level. Often three generations of a family lived in the same house. So with grandparents, parents, and children, an Israelite home held between eight and fifteen people, plus livestock. They certainly didn't have the same sense of privacy and personal space that we have in modern society.

Remains of an Israelite home at Gezer, Israel (photo by Cyndi Parker)

While we think about the house and family, remember that Israelite society was built around honor, family, land, and narrative. Individuals were known as a part of a family and, therefore, any decision made by an individual affected the whole family. As we study more about Lady Wisdom, be thinking about how the individuals mentioned in the Bible passage influence others around them.

Women in Proverbs

In the book of Proverbs, we meet several complex women described as:

- Wisdom (Prov. 1:20–33; 3:13–26; 4:5–9; 8:1–36)
- Wife (Prov. 5:18–19; 12:4; 31:10–31)
- Mother/teacher (Prov. 1:8; 6:20; 23:22, 25)
- Sister (Prov. 7:4)
- Folly (Prov. 9:13)
- Adulterer or wayward woman (Prov. 2:16–17; 5:3–6; 6:24–29; 7:5, 10–23)
- Sage (Prov. 14:1)

Most of these female figures are in chapters 1–9 and 31. These opening and closing chapters paint portraits before our eyes of normal people acting within normal society. The presence of women in these chapters anchors the whole book in the common Israelite community. These are the wise words that are shared by mothers and fathers to their children. These vignettes push us to consider how wisdom is lived out in the lives of individuals and in the community.

Geography

The setting for Proverbs 9 is vague—an unnamed city, a house, a street. Yet they are also familiar, so that everyone can relate to the lesson.

As you read the passage, you may have noticed the attention placed on food. Ancient Israelites normally ate simple, mostly vegetarian meals. Their primary ingredients were grain, wine, oil, vegetables, and spices. They harvested their food from small family plots of land, and if they owned sheep or goats, they let them graze in the wilderness beyond the agricultural fields. Families rarely slaughtered their animals, unless there was an important feast or if they had to thin out the flock. Sheep and goats were used for their milk, fleece or hair, and also dung, which was dried out and used for fuel.

Figs, grapes, barley, wheat, olives, dried dates, and pomegranates

People in Old Testament times did not have easy access to water. Only a few communities were located near a fresh water spring. Many others relied on drawing water from a well or collecting rainwater through the wet season and rationing the collection through the dry season. People had to develop clever agricultural practices and be smart about which plants grew in their drought-prone landscape. It's fair to say that the land was thirsty, and the people were thirsty.

Narrative

The middle verses of Proverbs 9 (verses 7–12) are the heart of this chapter. They contain the primary lesson: "The fear of the Lord is the beginning of wisdom, and knowledge of the Holy One is understanding" (verse 10). *Fear,* as it's used in this verse, is not the emotion that makes your knees knock together or chills go down your spine. The fear of God is reverence and awe for God's power, generosity, and instruction. Fear of God leads to obedience (see Deut. 6:1–2, 24; Ps. 33:8–9). Phrases like "the fear of the Lord" can be grand and a little ambiguous, so the writer of Proverbs 9 brings this teaching to life with two scenes on either side of this wise nugget. Let's look first at Lady Wisdom and then her opposite in Dame Folly.

Proverbs 9

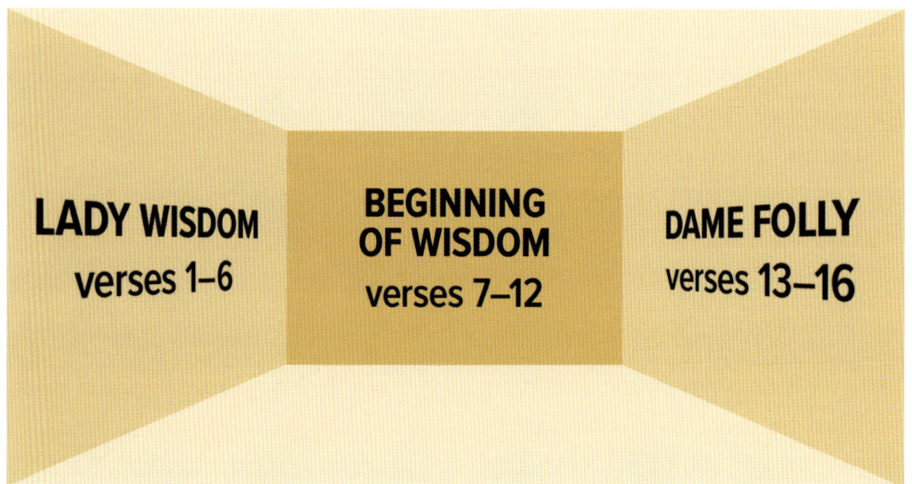

Wisdom

Lady Wisdom is introduced through a long list of action verbs. First we see her house and are told she "set up" (or "hewed out") seven pillars (Prov. 9:1). Why the detail of seven pillars?

- It could be a reference to the seven days of creation (Gen. 1); after all, Wisdom says creation was her project (Prov. 8).
- There were seven-pillared temples throughout the ancient world. Maybe the verse hints that her house is a temple.

- Ancient Israelites had pillared houses. The detail of seven pillars may suggest that Wisdom built a large house with ample space for all people.

In Proverbs 9:2, we see Wisdom's menu. Some Bible translations say she "prepared her meat," but a more literal translation of the Hebrew is that she "slaughtered her beast." Do those two phrases have different connotations to you? They mean the same thing, but slaughtering a beast seems so much more involved. If you were an ancient Israelite, do you know why you would be so excited about this meal? Meat is on the menu!

Wisdom also mixes wine and sets her table. She sends out servants, and she herself goes into the community to offer an invitation. Look at who she addresses in verse 4. She invites the *peti* (*simple* or *naive*) to enter her home, and eat her food and drink her wine. She asks them to leave their simple ways behind, find life, and walk in the way of insight. Accepting her invitation transforms the life of the individual. But remember the community mindset; when the individual experiences the benefits of wisdom and has a changed life, the health of the whole community is strengthened.

Folly

We are introduced to Dame Folly in verse 13.

> *Folly is an unruly woman; she is simple and knows nothing.*

She is described in the first half of the verse as *unruly.* What about the second half? What word does your Bible translation use: *simple, naive, gullible?* In Hebrew, the word is *petayyut*, which is a form of the same word to describe the people wisdom invites to her home in verse 4 (*peti*). This implies that Folly is one of the naive who should have responded to Wisdom's invitation, but who chose to remain in a state of foolishness.

What about her actions? We saw that Lady Wisdom was actively and personally involved in setting up her banquet. But Dame

Folly sits (verse 14). That is it. From her seated position, she offers an invitation to the community. At a quick glance, she seems to offer the same kind of hospitality as Wisdom, but when we pay attention to the details, we see this is not true.

Folly invites those who are naive into her house.

> *Stolen water is sweet; food [bread] eaten in secret is delicious! (Prov. 9:17)*

There is no care in the preparation of even these few items. Even worse, the water is stolen. There is no scenario in which this simple fact would not be highly offensive among an ancient Israelite community that was always worried about water. And Folly's bread that was normally made as a communal activity among women is eaten in secret.

To make matters worse, those who are invited do not understand the effects of the meal. They are swallowed up by the grave (verse 18). An ancient Israelite house was a place of safety and nourishment, but Folly's home is a place where community members die.

What Is Folly?

Folly (*sikluth* in Hebrew) is also translated as "foolishness." In the book of Proverbs, being a "fool" doesn't mean acting silly or being a class clown. Nor does it necessarily mean being naive or young and inexperienced, which is more characteristic of the "simple." Instead, folly refers to an obstinate heart opposed to the things of God (Prov. 13:9). The fool and Dame Folly all represent a path that eventually leads to ruin. Wisdom, by contrast, is the path toward holiness and a heart in tune with the things of God (Prov. 3:13).

"The fear of the LORD is the beginning of wisdom" (Prov. 9:10). Honoring, listening to, and respecting our God is where wisdom starts. You, the listener or the student of this passage in Proverbs, have a choice to reject or embrace the teaching. You can be a scoffer or a wise woman.

But what does all of this mean? The portraits of wisdom and folly in Proverbs 9 serve as the examples rooted in daily life. They each seek devotees to their ways. Accepting God's teaching is like choosing to feast at a generous table and receive life offered to us. Rejecting God's teaching is like eating stolen food, not only taken at the expense of the community, but also leading toward death.

This passage in Proverbs ends abruptly, leaving us with the choice before us that we are asked to make. Between wisdom and folly, which invitation will you accept?

Life Application Questions

1. If you tried to modernize the meals Wisdom and Folly offered, what food and drink would be on the menu?

2. Imagine yourself in the scene with Lady Wisdom. Take time to picture yourself walking through her house and watching the meal preparation. What emotions does this bring up for you? What impacts you when you place yourself in the narrative?

3. Does your family or community have wise sayings that are passed down through the generations? What are they? What are their origins?

4. What women do you go to for wise advice? How would you describe these women who play such an important role in your life?

5. Is there a decision you need to make or an area in your life where you need guidance? Journal about that and then place it before God in prayer.

6. Consider all the women you've learned about in these past six sessions. If you could join these diverse women in a group conversation, what would you want to ask them? How might they talk about God? Is there a woman you would try to pull aside to have a private conversation with?

Prayer

God of Wisdom, Righteousness, and Justice.

God of hospitality and love.

God of the hungry and of those pushed aside and forgotten.

God of the women who seek your face and of the naive who do not know how much they need you.

Remember your daughters today.

Remember those who hunger for your provision.

Remember the women you equip to be teachers of wisdom.

Remember those who proactively welcome others into your presence.

Remember us when we stray off the path but desperately want to return.

Remember your daughters today.

Notes

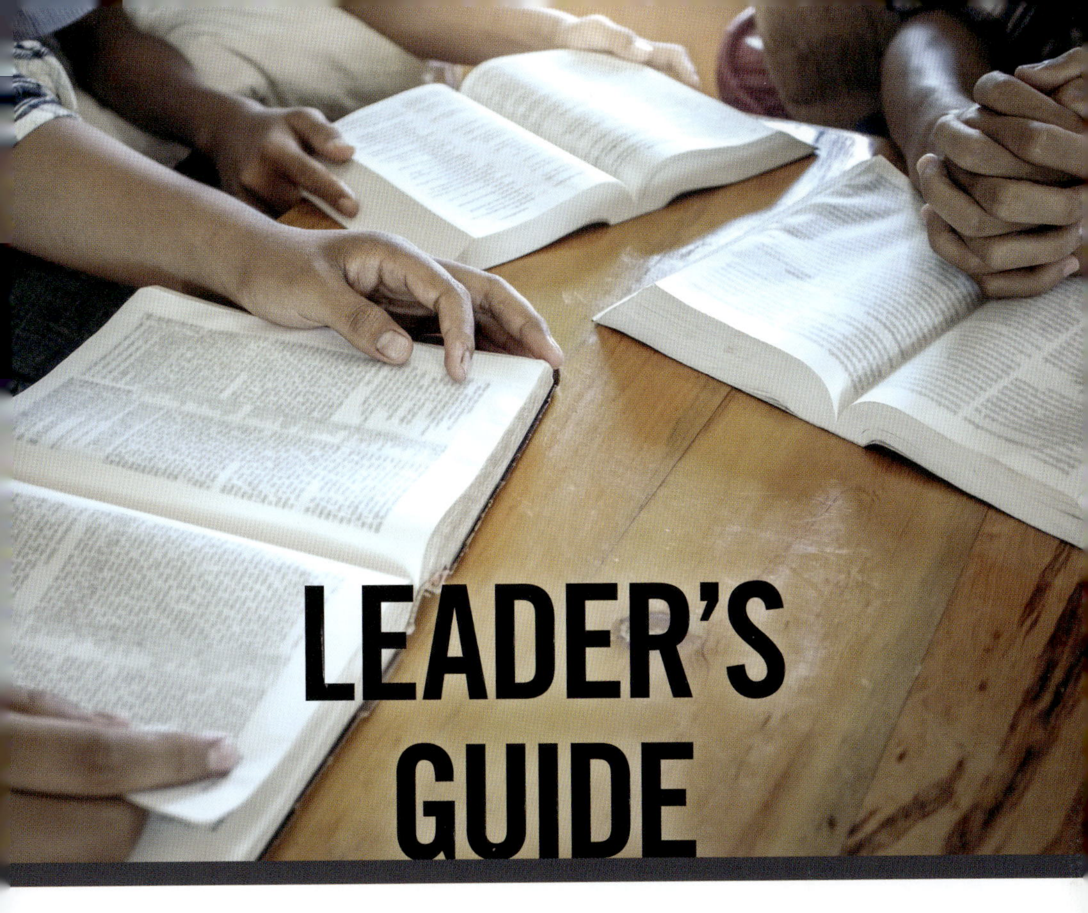

"Encourage one another and build each other up."

1 THESSALONIANS 5:11

Leader's Guide

Congratulations! You've either decided to lead a Bible study, or you're thinking hard about it. Guess what? God does big things through small groups. When his people gather together, open his Word, and invite his Spirit to work, their lives are changed!

Do you feel intimidated yet?

Be comforted by this: even the great apostle Paul felt "in over his head" at times. When he went to Corinth to help people grasp God's truth, he admitted he was overwhelmed: "I came to you in weakness with great fear and trembling" (1 Corinthians 2:3). Later he wondered, "Who is adequate for such a task as this?" (2 Corinthians 2:16 NLT).

Feelings of inadequacy are normal; every leader has them. What's more, they're actually healthy. They keep us dependent on the Lord. It is in our times of greatest weakness that God works most powerfully. The Lord assured Paul, "My grace is sufficient for you, for my power is made perfect in weakness" (2 Corinthians 12:9).

The Goal

What is the goal of a Bible study group? Listen as the apostle Paul speaks to Christians:

- "Oh, my dear children! I feel as if I'm going through labor pains for you again, and they will continue until *Christ is fully developed in your lives*" (Galatians 4:19 NLT, emphasis added).
- "For God knew his people in advance, and he chose them *to become like his Son*" (Romans 8:29 NLT, emphasis added).

Do you see it? God's ultimate goal for us is that we would become like Jesus Christ. This means a Bible study is not about filling our heads with more information. Rather, it is about undergoing transformation. We study and apply God's truth so that it will reshape our hearts and minds, and so that over time, we will become more and more like Jesus.

Paul said, "The purpose of my instruction is that all believers would be filled with love that comes from a pure heart, a clear conscience, and genuine faith" (1 Timothy 1:5 NLT).

This isn't about trying to "master the Bible." No, we're praying that God's Word will master us, and through humble submission to its authority, we'll be changed from the inside out.

Your Role

Many group leaders experience frustration because they confuse their role with God's role. Here's the truth: God alone knows our deep hang-ups and hurts. Only he can save a soul, heal a heart, fix a life. It is God who rescues people from depression, addictions, bitterness, guilt, and shame. We Bible study leaders need to realize that *we can't do any of those things.*

So what can we do? More than we think!

- We can pray.
- We can trust God to work powerfully.
- We can obey the Spirit's promptings.
- We can prepare for group gatherings.
- We can keep showing up faithfully.

With group members:

- We can invite, remind, encourage, and love.
- We can ask good questions and then listen attentively.
- We can gently speak tough truths.
- We can celebrate with those who are happy and weep with those who are sad.
- We can call and text and let them know we've got their back.

But we can never do the things that only the Almighty can do.

- We can't play the Holy Spirit in another person's life.
- We can't be in charge of outcomes.
- We can't force God to work according to our timetables.

And one more important reminder: besides God's role and our role, group members also have a key role to play in this process. If they don't show up, prepare, or open their hearts to God's transforming truth, no life change will take place. We're not called to manipulate or shame, pressure or arm twist. We're not to blame if members don't make progress—and we don't get the credit when they do. We're mere instruments in the hands of God.

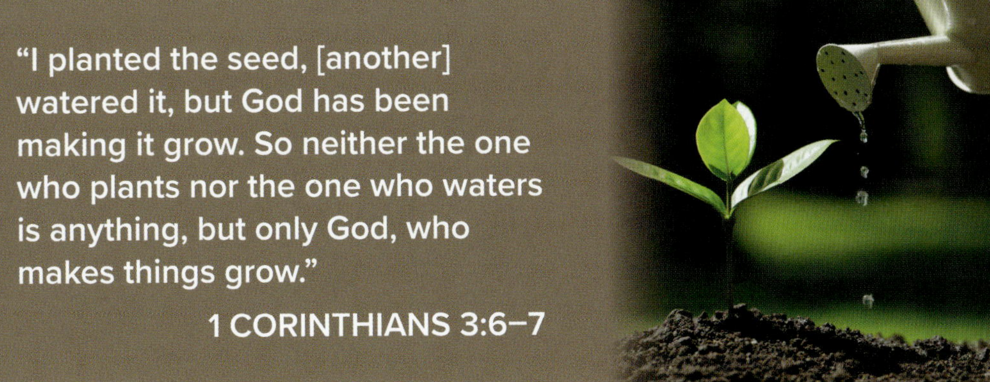

Leader Myths and Truths

Many people assume that a Bible study leader should:

- Be a Bible scholar.
- Be a dynamic communicator.
- Have a big, fancy house to meet in.
- Have it all together—no doubts, bad habits, or struggles.

These are myths—even outright lies of the enemy!

Here's the truth:

- God is looking for humble Bible students, not scholars.
- You're not signing up to give lectures, you're agreeing to facilitate discussions.
- You don't need a palace, just a place where you can have uninterrupted discussions. (Perhaps one of your group members will agree to host your study.)
- Nobody has it all together. We are all in process. We are all seeking to work out "our salvation with fear and trembling" (Philippians 2:12).

As long as your desire is that Jesus be Lord of your life, God will use you!

Some Bad Reasons to Lead a Group

- You want to wow others with your biblical knowledge.
  "Love . . . does not boast, it is not proud" (1 Corinthians 13:4).

- You're seeking a hidden personal gain or profit.
  "We do not peddle the word of God for profit" (2 Corinthians 2:17).

- You want to tell people how wrong they are.
  "Do not condemn" (Romans 2:1).

- You want to fix or rescue people.
  "It is God who works in you to will and to act" (Philippians 2:13).

- You're being pressured to do it.
  "Am I now trying to win the approval of human beings, or of God?" (Galatians 1:10).

A Few Do's

✔ Pray for your group.

Are you praying for your group members regularly? It is the most important thing a leader can do for his or her group.

✔ Ask for help.

If you're new at leading, spend time with an experienced group leader and pick his or her brain.

✔ Encourage members to prepare.

Challenge participants to read the Bible passages and the material in their study guides, and to answer and reflect on the study questions during the week prior to meeting.

✔ Discuss the group guidelines.

Go over important guidelines with your group at the first session, and again as needed if new members join the group in later sessions. See the *Group Guidelines* at the end of this leader's guide.

✔ Share the load.

Don't be a one-person show. Ask for volunteers. Let group members host the meeting, arrange for snacks, plan socials, lead group prayer times, and so forth. The old saying is true: Participants become boosters; spectators become critics.

✔ Be flexible.

If a group member shows up in crisis, it is okay to stop and take time to surround the hurting brother or sister with love. Provide a safe place for sharing. Listen and pray for his or her needs.

✔ Be kind.

Remember, there's a story—often a heart-breaking one—behind every face. This doesn't *excuse* bad or disruptive behavior on the part of group members, but it might *explain* it.

A Few Don'ts

✘ Don't "wing it."

Although these sessions are designed to require minimum preparation, read each one ahead of time. Highlight the questions you feel are especially important for your group to spend time on.

✘ Don't feel ashamed to say, "I don't know."

Disciple means "learner," not "know-it-all."

✘ Don't feel the need to "dump the truck."

You don't have to say everything you know. There is always next week. A little silence during group discussion time, that's fine. Let members wrestle with questions.

✘ Don't put members on the spot.

Invite others to share and pray, but don't pressure them. Give everyone an opportunity to participate. People will open up on their own time as they learn to trust the group.

✘ Don't go down "rabbit trails."

Be careful not to let one person dominate the time or for the discussion to go down the gossip road. At the same time, don't short-circuit those occasions when the Holy Spirit is working in your group members' lives and therefore they *need* to share a lot.

✘ Don't feel pressure to cover every question.

Better to have a robust discussion of four questions than a superficial conversation of ten.

✘ Don't go long.

Encourage good discussion, but don't be afraid to "rope 'em back in" when needed. Start and end on time. If you do this from the beginning, you'll avoid the tendency of group members to arrive later and later as the season goes on.

How to Use This Study Guide

Many group members have busy lives—dealing with long work hours, childcare, and a host of other obligations. These sessions are designed to be as simple and straightforward as possible to fit into a busy schedule. Nevertheless, encourage group members to set aside some time during the week (even if it's only a little) to pray, read the key Bible passage, and respond to questions in this study guide. This will make the group discussion and experience much more rewarding for everyone.

Each session contains four parts.

Read It

The *Key Bible Passage* is the portion of Scripture everyone should read during the week before the group meeting. The group can read it together at the beginning of the session as well.

The *Optional Reading* is for those who want to dig deeper and read lengthier Bible passages on their own during the week.

Know It

This section encourages participants to reflect on the Bible passage they've just read. Here, the goal is to interact with the biblical text and grasp what it says. (We'll get into practical application later.)

Explore It

Here group members can find background information with charts and visuals to help them understand the Bible passage and the topic more deeply. They'll move beyond the text itself and see how it connects to other parts of Scripture and the historical and cultural context.

Live It

Finally, participants will examine how God's Word connects to their lives. There are application questions for group discussion or personal reflection, practical ideas to apply what they've learned from God's Word, and a closing thought and/or prayer. (Remember, you don't have to cover all the questions or everything in this section during group time. Focus on what's most important for your group.)

Celebrate!

Here's an idea: Have a plan for celebrating your time together after the last session of this Bible study. Do something special after your gathering time, or plan a separate celebration for another time and place. Maybe someone in your group has the gift of hospitality—let them use their gifting and organize the celebration.

	30-MINUTE SESSION	60-MINUTE SESSION
READ IT	Open in prayer and read the *Key Bible Passage.* 5 minutes	Open in prayer and read the *Key Bible Passage.* 5 minutes
KNOW IT	Ask: "What stood out to you from this Bible passage?" 5 minutes	Ask: "What stood out to you from this Bible passage?" 5 minutes
EXPLORE IT	Encourage group members to read this section on their own, but don't spend group time on it. Move on to the life application questions.	Ask: "What did you find new or helpful in the *Explore It* section? What do you still have questions about?" 10 minutes
LIVE IT	Members voluntarily share their answers to 3 or 4 of the life application questions. 15 minutes	Members voluntarily share their answers to the life application questions. 25 minutes
PRAYER & CLOSING	Conclude with a brief prayer. 5 minutes	Share prayer requests and praise reports. Encourage the group to pray for each other in the coming week. Conclude with a brief prayer. 15 minutes

	90-MINUTE SESSION
	Open in prayer and read the *Key Bible Passage.* 5 minutes
	• Ask: "What stood out to you from this Bible passage?" • Then go over the *Know It* questions as a group. 10 minutes
	• Ask: "What did you find new or helpful in the *Explore It* section? What do you still have questions about?" • Here, the leader can add information found while preparing for the session. • If there are questions or a worksheet in this section, go over those as a group. 20 minutes
	• Members voluntarily share their answers to the life application questions. • Wrap up this time with a closing thought or suggestions for how to put into practice in the coming week what was just learned from God's Word. 30 minutes
	• Share prayer requests and praise reports. • Members voluntarily pray during group time about the requests and praises shared. • Encourage the group to pray for each other in the coming week. 25 minutes

Group Guidelines

This group is about discovering God's truth, supporting each other, and finding growth in our new life in Christ. To reach these goals, a group needs a few simple guidelines that everyone should follow for the group to stay healthy and for trust to develop.

1. **Everyone agrees to make group time a priority.**
   We understand that there are work, health, and family issues that come up. So if there is an emergency or schedule conflict that cannot be avoided, be sure to let someone know that you can't make it that week. This may seem like a small thing, but it makes a big difference to your other group members.

2. **What is said in the group stays in the group.**
   Accept it now: we are going to share some personal things. Therefore, the group must be a safe and confidential place to share.

3. **Don't be judgmental, even if you strongly disagree.**
   Listen first, and contribute your perspective only as needed. Remember, you don't fully know someone else's story. Take this advice from James: "Be quick to listen, slow to speak, and slow to become angry" (James 1:19).

4. **Be patient with one another.**
   We are all in process, and some of us are hurting and struggling more than others. Don't expect bad habits or attitudes to disappear overnight.

5. **Everyone participates.**
   It may take time to learn how to share, but as you develop a trust toward the other group members, take the chance.

If you struggle in any of these areas, ask God's help for growth, and ask the group to help hold you accountable. Remember, you're all growing together.

Notes

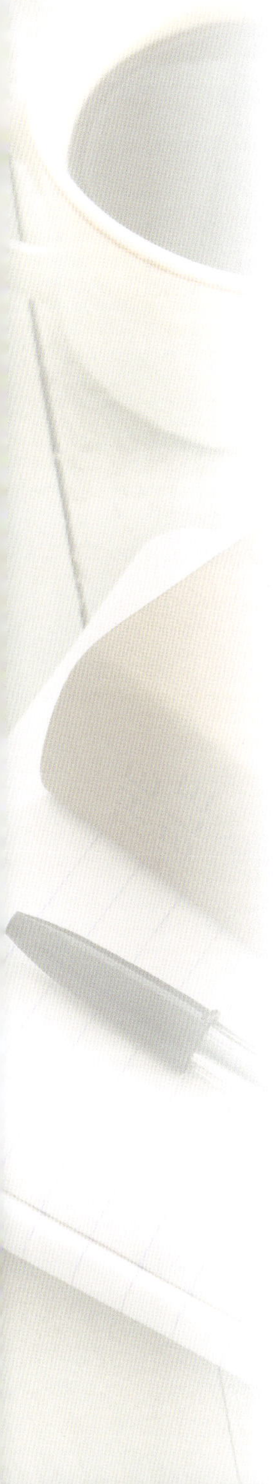

ROSE VISUAL BIBLE STUDIES

6-Session Study Guides for Personal or Group Use

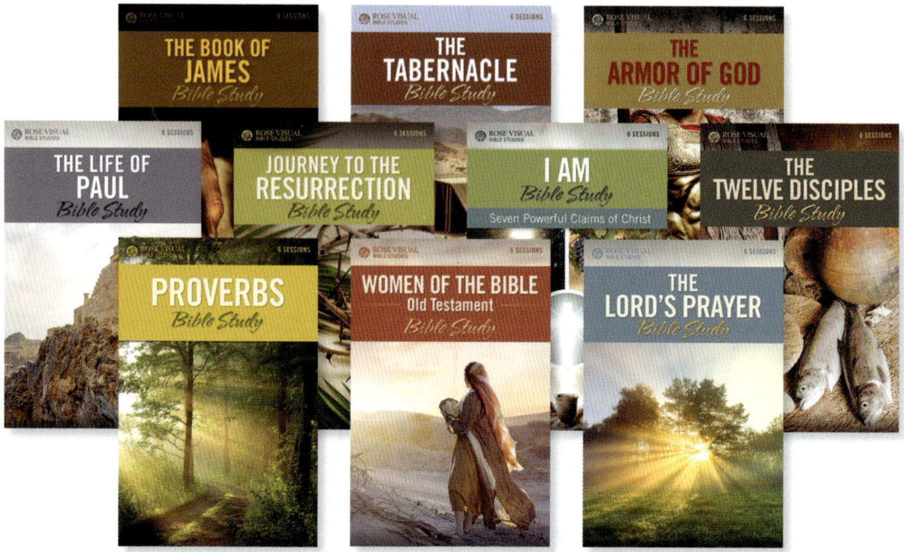

THE BOOK OF JAMES
Find out how to cultivate a living faith through six tests of faith.

THE TABERNACLE
Discover how each item of the tabernacle foreshadowed Jesus.

THE ARMOR OF GOD
Dig deep into Ephesians 6 and learn the meaning of each piece of the armor.

THE LIFE OF PAUL
See how the apostle Paul persevered through trials and proclaimed the gospel.

JOURNEY TO THE RESURRECTION
Renew your heart and mind as you engage in spiritual practices. Perfect for Easter.

I AM
Know the seven powerful claims of Christ from the gospel of John.

THE TWELVE DISCIPLES
Learn about the twelve men Jesus chose to be his disciples.

PROVERBS
Gain practical, godly wisdom from the book of Proverbs.

WOMEN OF THE BIBLE: OLD TESTAMENT
Journey through six inspiring stories of women of courage and wisdom.

THE LORD'S PRAYER
Deepen your prayer life with the seven petitions in the Lord's Prayer.

www.hendricksonrose.com